EFFECTIVE LISTENING

EFFECTIVE LISTENING

Developing Dialogue Skills
for the Counseling Interview

MIKE GREEN

Effective Listening

Effective Listening, Second Edition

Copyright © 1996, 2003 Mike Green

Published by:
> Proclaiming His Word Publications
> PO Box 2339
> Santa Rosa Beach, FL 32459
> 877-214-8076
> www.phw.org

Editorial Consultant: Chester D. Kylstra

First Edition, 1996.   ISBN 0-9649398-4-3
Second Edition, 2003   ISBN 0-9649398-7-8

Table of Contents

Acknowledgments

I wish to express my sincere appreciation to those who have helped me get this far in my own healing journey. Many, many people have inspired, encouraged, instructed, and challenged me during the last twelve years of my life in Christ. Their wise counsel and persistent patience ignited a fire of desire in me to help heal the brokenhearted and set the captives free.

Foremost among these people is my loving wife Michele. Her sacrificial dedication through years of trials cannot be praised enough. She is my best friend and strongest supporter and I love her more than I can express. Our faithful friends, Bruce and Carol Barnes have been there time and again, standing in the gap. Thanks guys. Chester and Betsy Kylstra are still my role models. They have consistently demonstrated what being a disciple of Jesus Christ looks like. I thank them for *Restoring The Foundations*. They have graciously provided many opportunities for me to learn and to teach. Gary Moon and Harold Rhoades, who worked with me as a graduate student at Regent University, challenged and inspired me with their wisdom and compassion. Marilyn Akerson listened effectively while I worked through my own stuff. Drew McHolm, Frank Longino, and Joe Sheehan spoke truth into my life at a crucial time.

And truly many, many more have blessed me along the way. To all of you I extend my heart-felt gratitude. I love you.

Preface for 2003 Edition

Since the first printing of Effective Listening in 1996 I have received much feedback from many satisfied readers. Most of it has been very positive. Often students tell me they feel better prepared to counsel. They tell me they have helped their clients tell their story better by implementing the skills discussed in the book. Comments like these are very satisfying. On rare occasions though I receive negative feedback about the book. This usually consists of asking why I did not go into more detail, or why I didn't give more practical examples of how I use the skills in a real counseling session. Both are good questions. And though it was our original intention to keep the book concise we are now happy to introduce this new addition.

Therefore, in the new addition you will find more examples of how and when or where in the session to apply the various skills.

We have also included a **New Appendix** to give a brief history of the Christian Counseling Ministry. We hope you will find this history interesting. And we hope you who have answered the call to counsel will feel more in touch with those who have preceded you in this important ministry. It is our prayer that this little book will help you fulfill your call to assist the Holy Spirit in His work of healing the broken-hearted and setting the captives free. May all you do be done for God's glory and the benefit of everyone He directs to you for biblical counseling ministry.

Mike Green,
October, 2003

Preface

Why a book on listening? Isn't listening something we all do, all day long, all of our lives? Yes, of course it is. But how well do we do it? Is our listening really effective? As most of us can testify, there is often a big difference between what one person says and what another person hears! Often, in normal conversation there is a lot more going on than we realize! For the conversation to be meaningful there are many variables to be considered that will have a profound effect on the quality of that conversation. Listed below are a few of the variables to be considered during any discussion.

1. What I actually said.
2. What I really meant to say.
3. What I tried to avoid saying.
4. What you heard.
5. What you didn't hear.
6. What you thought you heard.
7. What you thought I meant.
8. What you said in response to all of the above.
9. What I then heard you say.
10. What I thought you meant.

And so on. Added to all of these variables are things like: my mood or attitude, your mood or attitude, the type of relationship (business, personal, formal, informal, superficial or intimate), the time of day, the location, the purpose of the conversation, and a host of other less obvious components. Considering all of this, one can quickly see that the ability to listen effectively is important in any conversation. But it is crucial to counseling conversation.

Chester and Betsy Kylstra discuss the role of the Holy Spirit in the counseling process in their book, *Restoring the Foundations.*[1] The Kylstras exhort Christian counselors to listen diligently to the Holy Spirit during each session. And listening to your counselee is just as important. Having worked with many counseling ministry trainees over the years who have little or no previous counseling experience we recognized the need for a manual discussing basic listening skills. We want to help you become the best listener you can be. Thus, with Chester and Betsy's encouragement, we present this small volume to help you increase your Effective Listening.

Mike Green
January, 1996

---

[1] Kylstra, Chester and Betsy. Please see Bibliography.

Effective Listening

Chapter I

Introduction

Jesus said, "He who has ears to hear, let him hear."
Matthew 11:15, Mark 7:16, Like 8:8.

His point was to remind us that often as we listen, we do not respond appropriately to what we hear. One of our primary functions as counselors is to hear more than the words our counselee says. Effectively listening includes responding to what he says in such a way that we encourage him to tell us everything.

Someone once said, "God gave us two ears and one mouth, therefore we should listen twice as much as we speak." This is good advice for anyone. And for those called to the counseling ministry it is critical. The Christian counselor's success rests on his ability to learn to listen to the counselee and to the Holy Spirit.

Effective Listening

Effective Listening, for the purposes of this discussion, refers to the process of engaging in meaningful dialogue with a counselee. Counselors should respond to the counselee in such a way that he is convinced the counselor understands him. Effective Listening includes both hearing and speaking. The dialogue cycle goes like this. First, the counselor asks questions that help the counselee talk about his personal thoughts and feelings regarding family members, friends, lovers, co-workers, and God. With the counselor's help he speaks

1

of his history, thoughts, beliefs, feelings, temptations, hopes, goals, and plans. Second, the counselor listens intently to the counselee's reply, gathering and remembering important information. Third, the counselor responds verbally to the counselee in such a way that he is reassured that he has been heard.

Establish Trust

Through this type of dialogue trust is established between the counselor and the counselee. Establishing trust should be one of the counselor's primary goals for the first session. By the end of the first session, the counselee should feel secure that he is in a safe place and that he has been heard. Thus, he is encouraged to continue telling the counselor his story.

Conversation or Counseling

Counseling interview/dialogue should not to be confused with a casual, every day conversation. It most definitely is different. Consider the following examples. In conversations with friends or family, we often respond to their confusion, complaints or hurts with advice. Often, we do this out of habit. If we think about it at all, we feel our advice will correct the problem. We do people a disservice when we mistakenly think we can correct their problem with words. Perhaps, we want so much to see their problem resolved that we believe our opinion will provide the healing we think they need. In such cases, it is possible we are concentrating more on our own need to be heard while overlooking their need to talk. This might be because their pain is too hard for us to bear because of our similar pain. So, to protect ourselves, we turn them off with trivial advice or "pat answers." In such cases the hurting person can leave our conversation feeling misunderstood or rejected! And in worst case scenarios, they may even feel guilty for making us feel bad. This is a terrible price to pay for sharing one's personal pain, and this is why counselors must learn to listen effectively.

Hearing and Healing

Those in church leadership all too frequently make the mistake of giving Biblical advice or a prophetic word when compassionate Effective Listening would be more helpful. In an effort to fix the situation or instruct the counselee they act too quickly. In our fast paced, high tech world we are taught to expect solutions to be quick and easy. But in the counseling room we must slow down if we are to listen effectively. We have heard more than a few counselee's say after a painful session of sharing, "Thank you for not giving me advice or some quick-fix scripture. That's what I expected from a Christian counselor."

Biblical advice is very necessary to the Christian's development. Speaking prophetically is sometimes needed and appropriate, but neither of these methods are as effective as they could be if the counselee doesn't feel he is heard by the counselor. The counselee will either ignore the advice or become more frustrated trying to apply it to his lifestyle. In every counseling session, the counselor should make sure his advice is not harmful in any way. A good counselor wants the counselee to leave the first session feeling heard even if he doesn't feel healed.

In the Fullness of Time

It can take a long time to collect enough information from a counselee to understand his problem completely. Time is very important when dealing with wounded, brokenhearted people. A counselee may have been hurt by people in spiritual authority who claimed to have his best interest at heart. Leaders who are sincere sometimes act too quickly, shutting down the one seeking to be heard. He may have been abused, rejected, or abandoned by family members who claimed to love him. A counselee who has been wounded by a member of church leadership might not be comfortable sharing his unchristian-like behavior or painful experiences with folks he doesn't trust. At times he may cover up the real issue until he feels safe in his relationship with the counselor.

We remember a man who said at the beginning of the third session, "I believe I can trust you, so now I'll tell you the real problem." It took time for him to feel confident enough in the counseling relationship to share the real issue! Expect to move slowly in the beginning. Even after trust is established and the sessions are moving along smoothly, take your time. If painful issues have been bothering a counselee for years don't mistakenly assume you will fix it in a few short hours of counseling. Experienced counselors have proven solutions. Ones they have used many times with good success. But the wise counselors have learned to save their solutions for the appropriate time. And that is when the counselee has been prepared to receive.

The Interview

The interview portion of a counseling session can be
the most important section. It is during this crucial time
that the counselor needs to hear clearly from both the
counselee and the Holy Spirit. The counselor wants to
obtain enough information from the counselee to correctly discern the real problem. He wants to look beyond the symptoms to uncover their roots. If he acts
too quickly, he may spend too much time ministering to
needs that are not critical, while overlooking the heart
of the problem. Doing so is like putting a band-aid on a
toothache. Therefore, it is essential that the counselor
develop Effective Listening skills.

Purpose

Before each session counselors should develop a purpose for the session. Ask yourself questions like; What
do I want to accomplish during this session? What are
my goals? What do I want to have achieved by the end
of the session? This will help you stay focused during
the session. It will guide your interview like a road
map guides your vacation plans. And without it, you
might just end up talking and sharing your wisdom with
the counselee. Which is, of course, not the purpose of
the counseling session.

The purpose of the book you are reading is to help you,
the Christian counselor, gain a better understanding of
the interview process. We will discuss some simple but
effective communication skills that will make you a
better counselor. Learning to use these skills will help
demonstrate to the counselee that you hear his pain and
can assist him in gaining the healing he desires. Remember, the counselor must provide the counselee with
a safe, secure environment. One in which he is free to

share his most private behavior, thoughts, and feelings. He must be reassured that the counselor is listening effectively. He must be confident he will not be criticized or judged by the counselor. When the counselor demonstrates this kind of listening skill, the counselee will openly tell his story. In the chapters that follow, we will present some simple but effective skills which help the counselee tell his story.

It is our hope and prayer that our heavenly Father will bless you with compassion, discernment, and wisdom as you assist Him in the two fold ministry of bringing healing to the broken hearted and setting the captives free.

Chapter II

Body Language and Affect

Did you know that a person gives you information about himself before he speaks a word? Yes, before he opens his mouth he speaks a language without words. His body acts as a silent voice and can tell you much about him. The posture he assumes when standing, sitting, or walking is a good indicator of such things as his present mood, his level of self-esteem, and his fears. This physical expression will also tell you how he feels about you. There are many subtle nuances of Body Language. Some of the more obvious postures are easily recognized.

For example, as a child, did you ever see one of your parents (or any authority figure for that matter) standing in front of you, feet spread, knees locked, hands on hips, eyes glaring, lips tightly pressed together? Not a pretty picture, is it? How did your Body Language respond? The impression a child gets when he sees such Body Language is that something very bad is about to happen. He may think there is a volcano rumbling inside the adult staring down at him and any minute it is going to blow up, spewing all manner of scalding hot verbal lava in his direction! Remembering such scenes may make us chuckle now, but it probably was not funny then. For those who have been on the receiving end of an angry parent's verbal or physical abuse, it may have been very frightening and painful.

Now look at a different scenario. This time it's two adults of opposite-sex sitting on the couch in the living room. Sitting sideways facing each other, they are close, but not too close. One leg is drawn up on the couch and one foot is on the floor. One arm is up on the back of the couch stretched out toward the other. The other person's leg and arm are in the same position and their fingers are slowly creeping toward each other. Eyes are darting here and there around the room and remaining fixed only for a moment at a time. This scene presents a quite different Body Language than that of the child and parent in the first scene. Most observers would agree the first scene generates fear. The second scene generates the "warm fuzzies."

Body Language in the counseling session can be just as revealing. How the counselee sits in a chair, where his feet are, where he directs his gaze, the position of his arms, and what he does with his hands, are just some of the many different and revealing ways a counselee can speak to the counselor silently. Let's look at some of these now and find out what they mean.

A word of caution before we begin; remember, in each counseling case we are dealing with unique individuals. Each has his own particular personality traits. That's because God likes variety. In His incomprehensible wisdom He decided no two humans should be identical. Each individual is but one shimmering facet of God's wonderfully endless range of variety and creativity. Therefore, when studying Body Language, be flexible. Don't place so much emphasis on the way a counselee sits that you overlook some of the more important facts revealed in his dialogue. Body Language is important but it is just one course of the entire delicious meal. It's good to be aware of it but don't judge a counselee's mood or attitude strictly on Body Language alone.

For the purposes of the counseling session there are two categories into which a counselee's Body Language will generally fit. They are, the Open Posture and the Closed Posture.

Open Posture

In the Open Posture the counselee's Body Language tells the counselor, "I am okay sitting here with you. I may be a bit anxious but I am not afraid." Typically a counselee displaying this attitude will sit comfortably, usually placing his back against the back of the chair or couch. Often his arms and hands will rest on the arms of the chair. Hand movements will be appropriate to the thoughts being expressed.

Feet
In the Open Posture men will often have both feet on the floor. Sometimes they will be flat on the floor sepa-rated comfortably with knees parted casually. Some-times they will cross their feet at the ankle. Women will place both feet on the floor, knees together. Often their knees, kept together, will be leaned to one side or the other with their lower legs in a diagonal position. If a woman is wearing slacks and she is comfortable she will cross her legs.

Men and women, if they are real comfortable, might pull one leg up on a couch or love seat and sit sideways. A very relaxed or confident person might even ask if it is okay for him to remove his shoes! We have had this happen on several occasions. This is a sign that the counselee is quite comfortable with the situation and is not in any hurry to leave.

Hands

In the Open Posture the counselee's hands will appear loose and relaxed. They will be used for describing or giving emphasis to many different thoughts. At one moment they may be holding on to each other and the next be waving around illustrating a point. If they are clasped together it is usually not too tightly, nor is it for very long. A counselee may even be free enough to place an arm on top of the back of a couch or love seat. These are all signs that the he is comfortable.

Eyes

Observing the manner in which the counselee uses his eyes is yet another way to discern his feelings. Our eyes are the most revealing signal of our mood, attitude, and feelings. To see the important place eyes have in dialogue, try having a conversation with a friend but ask them to keep their eyes closed. There will not be as much information exchanged as there would be if their eyes were open. In the Open Posture, if the counselee is relaxed, and not self-conscious, he will generally look directly at the counselor when he speaks.

The counselor should also monitor his own eye movement during the interview. If a counselee is comfortable enough to look the counselor in the eye the counselor must be sure he sends the same message back to the counselee. Try remaining fixed on his eyes as he talks. This demonstrates to the counselee that the counselor is interested in what he is saying. At first this eye-to-eye contact may be difficult. But with practice it will eventually become more comfortable. Watch closely to see opportunities to look away for a moment. Usually it's best to wait until the counselee glances away.

Closed Posture

Most counselees will be anxious during their first session. This is not unusual considering they are going to sit with someone they are meeting for the first time and talk about the most personal and private details of their lives! A counselee who is fearful or feels intimidated, shy or guilty, will often display the Closed Posture, at least at the beginning of the interview. Knowing this, during the initial interview the counselor's goal should be to help the counselee relax.

In the Closed Posture the counselee's Body Language might appear stiff or rigid. He may move very little during the interview. He will often be self-conscious about his hands. Or he may display restlessness. A finger might tap or a foot will shake.

A woman who feels vulnerable will keep her arms crossed, hands in her lap, sometimes with each hand gripping the opposite elbow. She might not sit back against the chair or couch. Her feet will be planted on the floor with ankles together.

A man who is resistant to the counseling process will often demonstrate this by keeping his arms crossed on his chest. He might go further by leaning back in his chair, as if trying to put more distance between himself and the counselor.

The Closed Posture says, "I'm anxious," "I'm afraid," or "I don't trust you, and I will reveal only a little bit at a time." The closed counselee tests the counselor's ability to listen closely to him. He wants to know if the counselor is interested in him as a person or just in his problem. We have noticed this tendency often with people who have been in counseling situations before. This can be especially true if a former counseling encounter did not go well. He will resist if he suspects the counselor is trying to get him to submit to his agenda. He will tend to be more concerned about the counselor's Body Language and eye contact than the counselor is of his. If the counselor challenges him by probing too deeply too early in the interview, he might try to move away in an effort to protect himself. As he can't move away physically, he will lower his eyes or turn his head to stare out the window. We have even had a counselee refuse to talk about a particularly painful issue. This isn't usually the case with a counselee who comes for Christian counseling, especially since he knows in advance the type of counseling being offered. However, it can still happen, so try not to act surprised if it does.

Establishing Rapport

Counselees demonstrating Closed Posture may have been so hurt by church leaders that they won't trust the counselor until rapport is established. To the closed person, a smile of reassurance is not always reassuring. Telling him to relax can produce the same frustration as does telling someone with laryngitis to speak up! The best way to help the counselee relax is to speak directly, clearly, and look him in the eye when addressing him. Also, it helps to use a tone of voice that demonstrates concern. An empathetic response is best. Don't try to talk down to an adult counselee as one might speak to a child. Stay relaxed, but be sensitive to the counselee's feelings of vulnerability. Try to show him you understand he is uncomfortable. In effect, try to win his trust. When a bond of trust is established the counselee with a Closed Posture will begin to let down his guard and will eventually open up to your compassionate questioning.

Combined Body Language

In addition to Open and Closed Postures there is another type of Body Language to be aware of: Combined Body Language. This refers to the combination of Body Language demonstrated by a couple during joint sessions. The counselor should be aware that a couple will provide information about their relationship by how and where they sit relative to each other. While observing their choice of seating and posture the counselor should ask himself some questions. Here are some examples.

1. Do they sit together on the same couch or in separate chairs?
2. If they sit in chairs are they separated by another piece of furniture?
3. Do they choose chairs facing each other rather than along side each other?
4. If they sit on the couch together do they sit at opposite ends of the couch? Or do they sit close with thighs or knees touching?
5. If they are holding hands is it because they are affectionate or is one of them fearful?
6. When one is talking does the other watch them?
7. How often does one interrupt the other?

You might notice one does all the talking. One of them might not say a word. Some couples will flow easily together as they tell their story. Observing their Combined Body Language, the counselor should ask himself why they react and respond to each other this way. Don't overlook these kinds of signs. Often they will tell you a lot about a couple. This kind of mental note taking is very important in assessing the condition of their relationship.

Affect

Eyes are mirrors of our emotions. Cover a man's face, all but his eyes, and his mood is still discernible. As much as eyes reveal alone, they also work as a team with the mouth, the position or tilt of the head, and other facial characteristics. While listening to his words, and reading his Body Language, also observe a counselee's over all Affect. It can be as revealing as his words and Body Language. Affect is a term that is often used as a synonym for feeling, emotion, or mood. However, it should be distinguished from the counselee's mood because it can change rapidly and several times during an interview even though his mood appears to stay the same. The counselor should pay particular attention to how and when the counselee's Affect changes. For example, when discussing his relationship with his children a man may display a happy or "up" Affect. When the conversation changes to his dysfunctional relationship with his parents his Affect may switch to sadness, pity, or anger. This change of Affect would be seen as appropriate.

Range of Affect

Range of Affect can also reveal a lot about a counselee. If his Affect is broad he will display a wide variety of facial expressions depending on the subject being discussed. If his Affect is constricted his expression may not change from happy to sad at times when the subject changes. An example of restricted Affect is if he appears withdrawn and unemotional even when he talks about what should be a pleasant event. Inappropriate or incongruous Affect is demonstrated when his expression appears to be in conflict with the subject being discussed. For example, a man chuckles when describing his father's emotional abuse or remains sad when describing his wife's love for him. We would say that his Affect is inappropriate or incongruous.

When observing the counselee's Body Language and Affect ask yourself questions about it. Why doesn't she look at me when she talks to me? Why does he sit that way? Why do they not touch each other? Why does she gently pull her hand away from his when he tries to hold it? Why does she always interrupt him? Why does he correct her on the details she is sharing? Why does she do all the talking?

Final Counseling Considerations

Monitoring Body Language and Affect may take some practice and experience to become natural for the new counselor. It might help to think of yourself as detective Columbo or Jessica Fletcher. But just do the best you can in the beginning. The Holy Spirit can be counted on to assist everyone who makes an honest effort to improve.

The key to a productive interview session is to remain focused. The heart of the interview session should be dialogue, with the counselee doing most of the talking.If the counselor notices he is doing too much talking, he should silently ask himself why. Is it nervousness? Is the counselee's story too painful? Is it too close to his own unresolved issues? Is he trying to give the counselee advice too quickly to ease his pain? Counselees who are reluctant to talk openly may require the counselor to talk more. But be careful with a counselee who talks easily and openly. He can disarm the counselor because he is giving information so effortlessly. Before you know it you can be enticed out of your counselor's role and into a casual conversation. All of a sudden you are talking to your counselee like you are old friends. Doing so might feel good but it can quite easily limit the amount of useful information you get from your counselee.

Remember to monitor your tone of voice. It might need to be adjusted depending on the type of counselee you are sitting with. A shy or guilty counselee needs to be reassured. One who is very talkative and who consistently wanders from the topic needs to be gently but firmly kept on track. People abused by authority figures need a softer tone. A pushy controller who is accustomed to getting his or her way through intimidation might need to be confronted firmly. When doing so remember to be polite. By monitoring his own input the counselor will be on his way to the goal of helping the counselee tell his story.

Observing Body Language and Affect will reward you with much additional information about your counselee. But it is just as important to ask yourself why a counselee acts the way he does. A lot is written these days about observing and controlling behavior. Christian counselors would do well to see behavior and Body Language as a symptom of a counselee's feelings about himself, the session, and the counselor.

The counselor should also be aware of his own Body Language and Affect. Both of these can have a significant effect on certain counselees. It's a good idea that the counselor monitor his posture as well during the session. It is not appropriate for the counselor to appear nervous even if he is. An anxious counselor can cause the counselee to doubt there is help for him here. Here are some things to look out for.

1. Try to avoid fidgeting in your chair.
2. Don't be overly expressive with your hands and arms.
3. Do not dominate the conversation.
4. Demonstrate the Open Posture and a calm, reassuring Affect.
5. Monitor your tone of voice to fit the counselee.

Clocks and Time

A three-hour session is typical when using the Restoring The Foundations Ministry method. This can be a very long time for a counselee! So, time is an important factor to keep in mind during the session. Becoming aware of the role eyes play during the interview can also help the counselor stay in touch with the passing of time. If done discreetly, a glance at a watch will not disturb the flow of conversation. Try not to be overly concerned with time though. Frequently checking a watch can silently tell the counselee that the counselor needs to be somewhere else. This can cause the counselee to feel "less important." Usually a peek at a watch is best done when the counselee is looking away. However, there is a simple solution to the question of clocks and the passing of time. Simply place a clock on a shelf, table, or wall behind the counselee. The counselee is unaware of it and the counselor can see it without disturbing the flow of the session.

Effective Listening

Chapter III

Dialogue Skills

Having discussed Body Language and Affect we will now turn our attention to the dialogue portion of the counseling session. At this point it is good to bear in mind that "Each person on the planet has a story and until you know it, you can't know him." Of all the many people you know, you really know the greatest number of them at a superficial level. You may even have lots of information about them. You know their name, address, phone number, age, children's names, children's spouse's names, etc. You may know them well enough to be aware of the pain they have suffered as adults. But you really don't know them until you know the pain they have suffered as children. Until you have that kind of information, you do not really know them. During the interview the counselor's job is to help the counselee share everything about his life. We counselors want our counselees to tell us all, or as we say, "the good, the bad, and the ugly." Because it is only when we know their story that we will know them. And not until then, until we know them at this very intimate level, we will be able to truly help them overcome the pain of their past and their fear of the future.

During the first sessions the counselor must gather information that will "fill in the blanks" left vacant during the application process. The goal of the first session is to help the counselee tell his story. Therefore, the counselee should do most of the talking. As a counselor learns to apply various Dialogue Skills during the interview he will be better prepared to empower the counselee to tell his story.

Effective Listening

In this section we will discuss the following Dialogue Skills: Open and Closed Questions; Empathy, Reflection, Agreement, and Silence; Paraphrase, Summary, and Self-Disclosure; Feedback and Confrontation. First we will define each skill and then we will give examples of how to use them in the interview.

Open and Closed Questions

During the interview try to remember the counselor's goal is to help the counselee tell his story. A key to help you stay focused during this dialogue process is remembering that you want to "get more information." In a casual conversation with a friend our tendency is to swap information on a particular subject. Something like batting a ball back and forth across a tennis court net. For example, first you say something about your game of golf and then I say something about my game of golf. Unless we have been trained we generally do not ask questions about what each other is saying. We just take the information at face value and respond with our own comments. In counseling dialogue the form of conversation is different. When a counselee gives us information we respond with a question so we can get more information about the subject we are discussing. During the interview we want to focus on getting more information and asking questions is the method by which we do so.

There are two different types of questions we can use to get more information. They are, Open Questions and Closed Questions. Open Questions draw the counselee out of himself and into the counseling dialogue. Closed Questions keep him closed off from the counselor and locked inside his personal prison.

Whenever possible the counselor must avoid using Closed Questions. Simply stated, a Closed Question is one which encourages either "yes" or "no" for an answer. In the effort to draw the counselee out and encourage him to tell his story, the counselor should ask questions that help the counselee talk. A Closed Question, being one that can be answered with a simple "yes" or "no," "closes" the counselee's opportunity to give more information. A Closed Question is closed because the counselee can answer "yes" or "no" without giving any personal information.

Look at this example. If the counselor wanted to gather information about the counselee's religious background he might ask, "Did you go to church as a kid?" The counselee could answer "yes" or "no" depending on his situation. Such a simple answer gives very little information about the counselee's religious background. And the counselor is left with no recourse but to ask something like, "Why?" or "Why not?" If he asks another closed question like "Did your parents want you to go to church?" The counselee may respond with "No." And the counselor must again ask the "why" questions. If this continues for very long the counselee will begin to feel like he is being interrogated. Most of us know there is a big difference between being interrogated and being interviewed.

The dialogue is quite different if an Open Question is used. Let's look at another example, "What was your church experience like when your were a child?" The counselee cannot answer "yes" or "no." To answer the question he must offer some personal information. It is easy to see that even if the counselee is reluctant to share, an Open Question empowers him to respond with more than "yes" or "no." Then, based on his response, the counselor will follow up with another question that allows the counselee to build upon what he has already shared. No matter how the counselee answers, the counselor remembers that he wants to "get more information" from the counselee. Once you learn this skill you will have no trouble helping your counselee tell his story.

Here's an example of how to use a line of Open Questions to get more information. Notice how the use of "what," "which," "how long," etc., help the counselee give the counselor important information.

Lor: "What is your favorite color?"

Lee: "Well, I like all shades of blue, but I guess my favorite color is sky blue."

Lor: "Sky blue, yes, that is a nice shade of blue. What is it about sky blue that makes it your favorite color?"

Lee: "Well, I've always been drawn to it. It seems so restful."

Lor: "How long has it been your favorite color?"

Lee: "Oh, gosh, a long time. Let's see, how long? Well my dad didn't care for it, he said it wasn't macho enough for me. But ever since I was a boy, I've just liked it."

Lor: "Ever since you were a boy. That's going back a ways then."

Lee: "Yeah, about forty years. I remember when I was about three or four, I had a blanket that I used to sleep with. It was sky blue too."

Lor: "Oh? Boy, that is a long time. What made it your favorite blanket?"

Lee: "Umm (chuckles self-consciously), I don't know really. I was just really into that blanket. I wouldn't sleep without it. I remember once when I was a little older my mom and dad got into a big argument because I still wanted to sleep with it."

Lor: "Really? Which one of them didn't want you to sleep with it?"

Lee: "Dad. (Affect gets gloomy) He thought it was sissy stuff. I didn't think about it that way. I guess mom didn't either, 'cause they really got into it that night."

Lor: "How old were you at the time?"

Lee: "Let's see, I must have been, well, we were still in that little house on Fulton Street, so, I was probably no more than six or seven."

Lor: "How did you react to the argument?"

Lee: "Well, it wasn't unusual for them to argue like that. I mean, they weren't real happy with each other. So, I guess I was probably impacted by it but not to any harmful degree."

Lor: "What do you mean your parents didn't get along real well?"

Lee: "They just didn't. They were constantly at each other. All the time."

Lor: "What do you suppose it was that made them treat each other that way?"

Lee: "Oh, I think they just didn't love each other. They got married too early. I think mom was seventeen at the time. Dad wasn't much older. Looking back now, I don't think they were ready for marriage."

As you can see the counselee is talking quite freely. Considering the first question was about his favorite color, he has given the counselor a lot of important information. This dialogue could go on for hours allowing the counselor to continue getting more information.

Effective Listening

Let's look at this conversation a little closer. Notice any Closed Questions? Nope, there isn't one. There are only Open Questions, and each one has a "bold" key word: "What," "How," and "Which." These are good words to use to get more information. Notice that the counselor asked a simple non-threatening first question. The subject was the counselee's favorite color, but look how much useful personal information the counselee offered. This is because the counselor responded to what the counselee said by asking for more information about what he said. The counselor did not offer his personal feelings on any subject, he didn't make lengthy comments, and he didn't give advice. Instead, he kept the counselee on track. He kept his focus, remembered his goal, and concentrated on the information the counselee was giving. The conversation just flowed along naturally. As it did it became increasingly more personal without becoming threatening. The counselee probably enjoyed giving the information. There's a good chance he felt good because someone was taking more than a casual interest in the details of his life. The counselor was doing his job, pursuing his goal and the counselee was feeling good about it.

Now look what could've happened if the counselor had started with the following Closed Question.

Lor: "Do you have a favorite color?"
Lee: "Yes."
Lor: "What is it?"
Lee: "Blue."
Lor: "Has blue always been your favorite color?"
Lee: "Yes."
Lor: "Did something happen to you to make blue your favorite color?"
Lee: "No."

Kind of boring, isn't it? It is a very impersonal conversation. It's more like an interrogation, and it doesn't give the counselor the information he needs to draw the counselee out. Such questioning could also make the counselee feel real uncomfortable. Questions that begin with "did," "do," and "can" are usually closed. They require an answer containing only the least amount of information. To get more information, try to avoid beginning a sentence with any of them.

Another word to use sparingly is, "Why?" Even though this little word can be useful in an Open Question, it can sometimes sound intimidating to a counselee. Think of the times authority figures have asked, "Why did you......" or "Why did they....." These kinds of questions can be interpreted as accusations by a counselee who has been mistreated by authority figures.

The "why" question can also have a damaging effect on a wounded counselee. It can be like asking him to explain behavior, events, or incidents that he truly does not or cannot understand. He might not know why something happened or why he did something. And asking him why someone else did something can be frustrating as well. Asking a counselee too many of these questions can cause him to become frustrated and even more confused. He could begin to feel picked on, guilty, or stupid.

If the counselor suspects the counselee doesn't clearly understand a situation or behavior, asking a "why" question can be used to confirm that suspicion and help him realize his lack of understanding. For example, "You said your father didn't like having you around when he was working in his wood shop, I wonder why?" This is a softer approach than asking simply,

Effective Listening

"Why didn't your father like having you around?"
Used this way a "why" question can be helpful. However, when working with wounded individuals the
counselor should choose wisely the right time to ask
"why?" For some people it can be a difficult question.

Remember, Open Questions draw the counselee out of
himself and into the counseling dialogue. Closed Questions keep him closed off from the counselor and
locked in his personal prison. For some, the thought of
coming out can be frightening. If a counselee has been
previously involved in a bad counseling experience, the
counselor needs to take some time to build rapport with
him. Bonding with the counselee is an important part
of every counseling relationship. This can be achieved
by drawing the counselee out with the effective use of
Open Questions.

Understanding the use of Open and Closed Questions
will prove to be a tremendous asset in counseling sessions. However, if this is new information for you,
practice is essential. Most of us are pretty poor conver-
sationalists. Our habit developed over many years of
trying to be heard is to bat the ball back and forth across
the conversational net. Try using Open Questions with
a friend. Next time they phone to tell you the latest
news respond by asking some Open Questions. If your
married, try it with your spouse in your next conversation. You will be delightfully surprised by their reac-
tion. In fact it may be hours before they take a breath!
Remember, there is nothing you do well that you have
not been doing for a long time. Using effective listening
skills is no different. Time given to practice will soon
have you mastering this simple but effective dialogue
skill. And your counselees will reward you for it by
giving you all the information you need to help them.

Empathy, Reflection, Agreement, and Silence

We now turn to four somewhat subtle interviewing skills. They are Empathy, Reflection, Agreement, and Silence. These four skills are subtle in that they are demonstrated as much by the counselor's Body Language as they are by his words. Body Language is important during the every counseling session and these four skills require equal parts of Body Language and Dialogue.

Empathy

The word "Empathy" has its root in the Greek word, pathos, which means "suffering." Two commonly used words from this root are, "sympathy" and "empathy." Sympathy implies a shared Agreement or harmony of another person's suffering. Sympathy in it's purest form can block the counselor's ability to help because he may become too involved with the counselee's pain.

Empathy is different. The counselor is empathetic by demonstrating that he understands the counselee's situation. Yet, unlike sympathy, the empathetic counselor can see and understand the counselee's suffering, but he is not incapacitated by it. A fitting analogy is the scene of a sinking sailboat on a park pond. The boat has sprung a leak. Sympathy compels a would-be rescuer to join the distressed skipper in his boat in an effort to help him bail out the water as the boat continues to sink. Empathy allows the rescuer to see the distress but keeps him in his boat, which is afloat and dry. From the safety of his position he is better able to assist with the rescue. The distressed sailor would much

27

more prefer to be pulled into the rescuer's dry boat than be joined in his own boat as it sinks.

During the early 1950's, psychologist Carl Rogers developed an entire counseling model[1] based on the counselee's need for Empathy. Rogers called this Empathy "unconditional positive regard" and taught that his non-directive, client-centered approach facilitated the counselee's discovery of his inner-personal wellspring of healing virtue. However, continued research has proven that as important as Empathy is to the therapeutic process, it is not a panacea. Said simply, "Empathy demonstrates that the counselor has a genuine and compassionate understanding of the counselee's situation." The empathetic response to the counselee during the interview gives him confidence that the counselor is capable of assisting him with his problem.

Reflection

Reflection is the term given to the "how" of Empathy. Listening quietly, displaying appropriate Affect, and asking Open Questions helps the counselee feel affirmed and accepted. As a result he feels empowered to tell his story. The empathetic counselor reflects on the counselee's story with phrases like, "Oh, I see." "Yes, I hear what you're saying," and "Gosh, that must've been awful." These phrases demonstrate to the counselee that the counselor not only hears his pain, but also feels it, as much as he can. However, the counselor shouldn't go overboard in this. The counselee knows the counselor cannot really feel the pain as he has felt it, so the counselor shouldn't try to convince the counselee otherwise. Doing so belittles the counselee's pain. Re-

---

[1] Rogers, Carl, Client-Centered Therapy: It's Current Practice, Implications, and Theory, Houghton Mifflin, Boston, 1951.

flecting appropriately is usually enough. Sometimes using this simple Reflection skill is all that is needed to encourage the counselee to share more.

If the counselor has had similar experiences, empathetic Reflection might come more easily. However, a wise counselor is on guard making sure he doesn't move from Empathy to sympathy. Remember, Empathy helps the counselor pull the counselee out of the sinking boat. Sympathy pulls the counselor into it! This is why it is so important for the counselor to have dealt with or at least be in the process of dealing with his own "stuff." Suppose a counselee is struggling to overcome spiritual abuse. If he relates an incident where someone in a church leadership position has broken confidence, and the counselor has had a similar experience, the counselor might become as angry as the counselee. At the moment the counselor loses his objectivity, he become useless to the counselee. At that point the counselor has ceased to be empathetic and has become sympathetic. And he has become useless to the counselee because the counselee sees the counselor is struggling with the same issue. The counselee may even feel bad for the counselor! Remember, to help the counselee, the counselor must resist the temptation to climb into the counselee's sinking boat.

Agreement

Agreement as it is used in the counseling process is one of empathy's team mates. It refers to letting the counselee know you hear his pain. By agreeing with the counselee the counselor acknowledges that what happened to the counselee was terrible, unfortunate, unfair, or whatever else is appropriate. Agreement is especially helpful when dealing with issues involving anger, guilt, and shame.

Effective Listening

A counselee who has been a victim of another person's anger, rejection, or abuse may mistakenly believe he has no right to feel the pain he really feels. Instead he feels guilty and sometimes gets the impression from well meaning friends and clergymen that he should "just let go and let God." Unfortunately, for the time being, he is unable to do that without the help of a skilled listener. He would love to let go of the past, and in fact, that may be the reason he has finally come for counseling, but he simply does not know how to do it. He feels guilty because he is angry. But he is angry because he has been hurt.

We remember one frustrated counselee who said with tears streaming down his face, "I'm broken, I'm angry, and I know I should be able to forgive, but my 'forgiver' just won't work." A counselee who has been abused needs to know that it's not a sin to hurt or to feel anger toward the ones who hurt him. Hurt, anger, and guilt are birds from the same flock. They fly together. Using Agreement can assist the counselee in discovering that it's okay to be angry. Anger is often a normal emotional response to an offense. It's not necessarily a bad emotion but we must learn to respond to it safely and appropriately.

Counseling helps the counselee confront his hurtful past in order to be healed of the pain that currently affects his present, and that if left unhealed may continue to disrupt his future. By allowing him the freedom to be angry in a safe, empathetic environment the counselor can teach the counselee to take control of his pain. When Agreement is used properly the counselor is not condoning the counselee's anger in order to feed it. No Christian counselor would ever even imply such a thing! The counselor knows forgiveness is the key to healing and to freedom from the pain of past offenses. However, until a counselee who is bound emotionally is empowered to feel his pain out loud, so to speak, he might never be able to resolve it in a healthy manner.

Agreeing with the counselee that the offense occurred, that it was awful, and that he has a right to feel angry, will usually empower him to let go of much of his guilt. Once free of the guilt he will find it easier to deal appropriately with his anger. Eventually he will become strong enough to comprehend true forgiveness.

Use Agreement whenever it is necessary. When the counselor understands the depth of the pain, guilt, anger, or shame a counselee is expressing and the reasons behind these feelings, he should tell the counselee. Expressions like, "I can see that really hurt you," or, "I can see why you are so angry (hurt, ashamed, etc.)," are very helpful. Agreement can simply be the word "Yes" following a counselee's remark. Sometimes just a subtle affirming nod of the head is enough to let the counselee know you hear him and you agree with him. Even though this is a simple expression it can encourage him to continue telling his story.

Silence

Wisdom is heard as often in a man's Silence as it is heard in his words. Silence is a rare commodity in the bustling, buzzing modern world. Who has time to be silent when there is so much stimulating stuff to hear, to see, to do, and to accomplish? In this hi-tech, fast paced society experiencing real soundless Silence is as rare as getting a good deal at a used car lot! Unless one climbs above the tree line, sails beyond the horizon, or sits alone in a sweat lodge, true soundless Silence is but a dream. With computers whirring, CD's and TV's blaring, AC's cycling, washers chugging, dryers tumbling, cars whizzing, aircraft droning, and neighbors playing, chopping, mowing, and sometimes even screaming, who can hear the Silence?

Silence does have a place in a counseling session. But what place does it have? After all, isn't a counseling session a conversation between two or more persons? Yes, it's true. Counseling is conducted through dialogue. But, there are special times in a counseling session when it is best to say nothing. A.W. Tozer[1] said of Silence, "It might well be a wonderful revelation to some Christians if they were to get completely quiet for a short time, long enough, let us say, to get acquainted with their own souls, and listen in the Silence for the deep voice of the Eternal God." I am amazed by the number of people I have known over the years that are never silent while they are awake! They seem to need some kind of noise droning in the background all the time. They listen to music while they eat, while they minister, during prayer times, in the car when they're driving, etc. They wear special listening devices to entertain themselves while they run in the country, ride their bikes, sail their sloops, and walk the dog. I have even met folks who can't go to sleep without a fan whirring, or music playing. I think many have forgotten how to be silent! They have lost touch with the therapeutic value of Silence.

There are rare, and wonderful moments during a counseling session when a difficult feeling has been expressed, a new revelation has been received, or a special insight has been gained. We say, "words cannot express the feeling I had when...." At such times Si-

---

[1] Tozer, A. W., The Knowledge of the Holy. Please see Bibliography.

lence is the only reasonable response. Usually both the counselee and counselor "feel" it. However, Silence can be frightening for those who rarely experience it. Dallas Willard[1] thinks, "We find Silence shocking because it leaves the impression that nothing is happening." In fact, sometimes in the counseling session more can happen when we do nothing than we realize.

This wonderful experience can take on many different forms depending on when and where in the session it occurs. Usually, though, when it happens it is unmistakable. During the Soul/Spirit Hurts ministry session of the Kylstra's RTF model[2] this phenomenon is frequently encountered. When it does occur it can be an indication that the Holy Spirit is doing something that the counselor can't do. The counselor must be sensitive to this so that he can "zip the lip and go with the flow." This is especially true for counselors who are unusually gregarious. Those who "have the gift of gab," or are fearful of Silence need to be wary of verbally "running over" the counselee during these quiet times. The Holy Spirit can be trusted to handle the counseling process during these special moments.

In some sessions the Silence is so enjoyable the counselor wouldn't want to disturb it, even for a week off with pay! During such times the counselor should just relax and let the Holy Spirit run the show. The counselee might cry or laugh. He might just sit and smile, or think. At this time the counselor's focus should continue to be on the counselee's behavior, Body Language and Affect. If he appears calm and comfortable, let the process proceed as the Holy Spirit directs.

---

[1] Willard, Dallas, The Spirit of the Disciplines, Harper and Row, 1988.
[2] Kylstra, Chester and Betsy, Please see Bibliography.

Effective Listening

A caution here about the use of Silence. If the counselor discerns after a few moments that the counselee is stuck in a difficult or frightening memory or re-experiencing pain that is too overwhelming, he should gently interrupt the Silence. He might simply ask quietly, "How are you doing?" If the counselee answers positively, give him a few more moments and then ask, "What's going on?" or, "What's the Holy Spirit showing you?" If he hesitates answering the first question then follow up on it more quickly with the second question. The Holy Spirit can work wonders during Silence. So, we don't want to prevent the counselee from receiving the benefit of a little discomfort during these periods of Silence. But by using wisdom a counselee will be helped, not hurt again, as a result of therapy.

Paraphrase, Summary, and Self-Disclosure

Now we come to three skills that will save you a lot of time, and help build trust with your counselee. Again, we don't want to overuse them, but they are very effective when used at the correct time.

Paraphrase

Paraphrasing is using carefully chosen words to restate what the counselee has said. It is used to clarify a lengthy dialogue. Using a Paraphrase tells the counselee you are tracking with him and you heard him correctly. Look at the following example.

Lee: "My father worked real hard to provide for us. He was always at work. I mean, we hardly ever saw him. Sometimes that was hard on mom. I could tell she didn't like it much. But, you know, what could we do about it? Complain? Get angry? That didn't change him. He still didn't do stuff with us that other dads did. So, mom and I just did the best we could."

Lor: "So because of your father's work ethic you and your mom were left alone a lot."

Lee: "Yeah, we were!"

In the dialogue above, the "bold" statement is a Paraphrase of the information the counselee gave the counselor. By rephrasing the information accurately the counselor told the counselee he heard him correctly. The counselor recognized the counselee's loneliness. The counselee agreed with the Paraphrase by saying, "Yeah, we were!" This exchange indicates that the

35

counselee and the counselor are communicating well. The counselee is talking and the counselor is listening.

This type of dialogue encourages the counselee to reveal more of his story because he's convinced the counselor is listening. At this point in the conversation the counselor could follow up with some Open Questions on several different topics. Here are a few examples.

1. How did your mom deal with her loneliness?
2. What do you think it was that made your dad spend so much time at work?
3. What did your mom and you do during all the time you spent alone?
4. What kind of effect did all that time with your mom have on you?

There are many paths this dialogue can take at this point in the conversation.

1. "How often did he overwork?"
2. "How many years did this go on?"
3. "How did his absence make you feel?"
4. "What did you think about it all?"
5. "What did you do to deal with your loneliness?"

The answer to each of these questions can be followed by another question.

There are two other helpful uses of Paraphrase. One effective use of this skill is to help keep the counselee on track. If a counselee has a tendency to wander, the counselor can say, "Now, you were saying......" Paraphrase is also an effective skill to gently probe a little deeper into a difficult subject. In the example above we could use Paraphrase to get more information on either the counselee's feelings toward his mother, his resentment of his father neglecting his wife, his frustration or anger resulting from his father's absence, or his mother's treatment of him, possibly as her surrogate husband. There are many avenues to pursue as we help him give us more information. Remember, during a counseling session it's okay for a counselor to become part detective.

Summary

Summary adds clarity and focus to a large body of information the counselee has given over a fairly long discourse. In this way it differs from Paraphrase. When a counselee has been talking nonstop for ten or fifteen minutes or longer it becomes necessary at some point to tie all the information up in a neat little bundle. Using Summary the counselor weeds through all the information and chooses the high lights. Then he offers the counselee a Summary to determine if the two of them are connecting. In a Summary there may be several major subjects reviewed. In a Paraphrase usually the focus is on one subject. So a Summary is really a long Paraphrase.

Using the dialogue about the man and his workaholic father from the section on Paraphrase the counselor could present the following Summary.

> "Excuse me, Bob, let me interrupt you for a second. You're giving me a lot of important information and I want to be sure I understand you. Let me share with you what I'm hearing and you tell me if I'm hearing you correctly. (Check his Affect as you begin to talk to make sure he's okay with your interruption.) You

say your father stayed away from home quite a
bit, due to his work. So, you and your mother
were forced to spend a lot of time alone together. You believe your father neglected his
responsibility to you and your mom by working so much. So what I think I'm hearing you
say is you're not only struggling with feelings
of rejection, you are also angry. Am I getting
this right?"

The counselee will either agree, disagree, or tell the
counselor if he missed anything. He might even add
something or emphasize something else. The use of
Summary will strengthen the rapport between the counselee and counselor by, once again, showing the counselee he has been heard. This skill takes some time to
do smoothly and we encourage you to practice with
people you talk with every day. Don't wait until you
get into the session to work on it.

Self-Disclosure

Some counselee's feel they are alone in their trauma.
They may believe no one has experienced anything like
they have. Sharing information from your life that is
relative to the subject being discussed by the counselee
can be helpful. It can make him see that others have
experienced situations or hurts similar to his own. Self-
Disclosure is a good way to bond with the counselee.
There are, however, some precautions to be considered
when using this particular listening skill.

While Self-Disclosure is an important dialogue skill, be
careful not to slip into it prematurely. If the counselor
is too anxious to bond he may rush too soon into sharing with the counselee his similar experiences. Counselors must use caution as it may appear to a wounded,

over-sensitive counselee that the counselor thinks his story is more important than the counselee's! Also, the counselor can diminish the counselee's ability to receive from him if the facts he shares are excessive or too personal. The main purpose of Self-Disclosure is to encourage the counselee, not to shift the emphasis to the counselor's story.

Here's an example from a casual conversation. Sue is telling Jane how restless her night was. Jane responds insensitively by saying, "Oh, I know what you mean, I didn't sleep a bit last night." Sue wonders if Jane heard her complaint and adds, "I mean I didn't sleep more than an hour during the whole night!" And Jane says, "Yeah, that used to happen to me all the time! You know what I do now when it happens?" And Jane proceeds to give Sue her fool-proof home remedy for insomnia! At this point Sue might be thinking. "Wait a minute here, I couldn't care less what you do about it, I'm trying to drum up a little Empathy!"

In a counseling session when a counselee is sharing a difficult or painful event he is looking for understanding and support. If the counselor starts Self-Disclosing too early, the counselee may feel his story is falling on deaf ears. He might even feel the counselor is in competition with him! When this happens the counselee gets the impression the counselor is more interested in his own perspective and couldn't care less about the counselee. The counselee may end up getting some advice, but there is the possibility he may leave the session feeling neglected.

Self-Disclosure is used best when it is used sparingly. Prior to using it the counselor should spend ample time getting more information, building rapport, and displaying Empathy. When this is accomplished the counselor will have earned the right to Self-Disclose. At that point he may share some of his story. It's best just to give the major details as clearly as possible. Include "feeling" words that are similar to the feelings the counselee expressed in the telling of his own story. It is not necessary to burden the counselee with too much detail though. Just tell the part of the story that relates to his situation. And the counselor should be sure to explain how the situation was resolved.

It is important that the counselor uses a variety of Self-Disclosure. One time a counselor may want to use Self-Disclosure to show the counselee that he has endured a similar trial, perhaps a divorce. Another time the counselor might want to identify with a specific mood or feeling the counselee has had, like being angry with a boss, a spouse, or a pastor. On rare occasions the counselor can use Self-Disclosure to provide hope in the midst of a hopeless situation, but be careful here. When a counselor is too optimistic too soon, he can make the counselee think he doesn't understand the severity of the counselee's situation.

A word of caution now for unseasoned counselors. As mentioned before, if the counselor's habit is to do most of the talking in any situation, he must learn the skill of "Zip the lip." The counselee has a need to talk, the counselor should listen. Self-Disclosure should not be used to dominate the conversation. Use Self-Disclosure sparingly and at the best possible times.

There are times during the session when it is best to avoid using Self-Disclosure. Avoid Self-Disclosure if the counselee appears overburdened or is struggling to get his own story out. At that point he is not able to receive from the counselor. Wait to use some Self-Disclosure after the ministry time when the mood is lighter and the counselee feels more hopeful. It is received a little more easily at this time. However, with the Holy Spirit as your guide you will soon learn to use Self-Disclosure wherever it will benefit the counselee.

In closing this section on Self-Disclosure try to remember to use it for bonding, building rapport, encouraging, and projecting hope. Avoid sharing "war stories" that discourage. For example, do not tell a counselee who has a family member fighting cancer that your Aunt Lucretia died of cancer two years ago! Self-Disclosure should never be used to create or feed hopelessness.

One final point to consider when using Self-Disclosure. A counselor should not use stories that are not his own. The purpose of Self-Disclosure is to encourage the counselee by showing him that the counselor has struggled also. Stories about third parties can illustrate similar situations but they don't have the same bonding effect of a personal Self-Disclosure. Under no circumstances should a counselor invent a story in an effort to help the counselee. In counseling, as in everything, honesty is the best policy. The rule is to use Self-Disclosure sparingly, honestly, and positively.

Feedback and Confrontation

Feedback and Confrontation are cousins in the Dialogue Skills family. They are related but different. They are both used for helping the counselee reflect on things like his attitude, mood, behavior, progress, and compliance or defiance. Of the two, Feedback is less challenging and more instructional. Very simply said, Feedback is an evaluative response.

Confrontation is more challenging than Feedback. One dictionary says Confrontation is "to come up against." Therefore, the counselor must use Confrontation with equal doses of firmness and compassion. A homiletics professor warned his aspiring young preachers about confronting from the pulpit. He said, "If you need to confront your congregation from the pulpit be sure you do so in love. If you confront them in love they will leave feeling instructed. If you confront them without love they will leave feeling they have been attacked, and they might not come back!" This is good advice for the Christian counselor as well.

Feedback
As was stated above, Feedback is the process of offering an evaluation of a counselee's input in the counseling session. There are many different ways to give Feedback. The counselor might simply compliment the counselee on his willingness to share openly some difficult experiences. Also, the counselor might respond to a question the counselee asks by offering his view of a situation or experience, or the counselor could verify or validate a particular insight the counselee has expressed. These are just three examples. The point is,

Feedback comes in many different forms and is used quite often in the counseling process. It doesn't require special training. Any time the counselor makes comments on the counselee's input he is offering Feedback. Always try to be positive and to encourage the counselee with Feedback.

Confrontation

If we think of people who have confronted us in the past we can quickly understand the difference between this dialogue skill and it's less forceful cousin, Feedback. Thinking about Confrontation usually brings thoughts of arguments, complaints, and criticism. No one enjoys being criticized. Even the term "constructive criticism" has an ominous sound to most folks. If the counselor is not careful, confronting a counselee with such things as his or her poor attitude, skirting of issues, denial, lying in the session and other equally "yucky" stuff can sound like criticism. However, there are times when the counselor must overcome his fear of being rejected by the counselee and confront anyway.

When a counselee keeps dancing around an issue by refusing to speak openly about it the counselor should Confront. The counselee must be shown that the counselor thinks he is avoiding the subject. A counselee may be so wounded he just can't openly admit his guilt in a particular situation. He might try to use words that indicate his responsibility but he ends every feeble admission of guilt with statements like, "but it wasn't that bad," or "but they had it coming to them," or "I don't think I really hurt them by saying that." The counselor may feel he is hearing a dual message. One part says, "I am guilty," and the other says, "I am not guilty." The counselor can express this confusion to the counselee by asking, "Are you or aren't you guilty?" If the counselee continues to avoid making a clear statement of his position, the counselor would do well to use Confrontation. Look at this example.

1. Lee: "Well, you know, my sister and I didn't really steal the money from my parents. It was ours anyway. We just sort of took it ahead of time. I'm sure it was okay."
2. Lor: "I'm a little confused by that last statement, could you explain it a little more clearly?"
3. Lee: "Well, you see, it was going to be part of our inheritance. We knew where it was kept and so whenever we needed some money we just took what was ours already. It was ours. And besides we knew they wouldn't miss it."
4. Lor: "You mean you took it before they gave it to you. And you didn't ask their permission?"
5. Lee: "Yes, why?"
6. Lor: "Well, it does sound a little like stealing to me."
7. Lee: "No, no, no, you misunderstood me. It was our money. It belonged to us and we would've gotten it eventually anyway. We didn't see it as stealing."
8. Lor: "Wait a minute. Let me see if I'm getting this. You took money that was being kept safely hidden away by your parents. You didn't ask them before you took it and you didn't tell them you had found it. And you don't think it was stealing. Is that right?
9. Lee: "Well, when you put it like that it does sound like stealing. But, we didn't do it like that. I mean, we weren't out and out stealing."
10. Lor: "Bob, when you say you weren't stealing but then say you didn't tell anyone or ask permission, I get the feeling that you know it was stealing but don't want to admit it because

you're ashamed of it. Are you ashamed of
what you and your sister did?"

11. Lee: "Yeah, I guess you're right. I am ashamed of
what we did."

In line 8 the counselor used a Summary to make sure he
and Bob were communicating. Bob agreed with the
Summary except for the statement about stealing. In
lines 1, 3, 7, and 9, Bob played down the concept of
stealing. In other words, he was stuck. The counselor
then confronted Bob clearly in line 10. The purpose of
the Confrontation was to get Bob to consider the possibility that he was ashamed of his behavior and just
couldn't admit that what he and his sister did amounted
to stealing from their parents. For the purpose of this
example Bob admitted his guilt. As uncomfortable as
the Confrontation can be for Bob (and perhaps for the
counselor) it allows Bob to admit his guilt and ask for
forgiveness. This is what healing is all about.

Care should be taken when using Confrontation. First,
the counselor needs to be absolutely sure his motive is
pure. That is, that he has the counselee's best interest at
heart. If he is not sure of this he should not confront.
Second, the counselor must know without doubt that
what he senses about the situation is true and that the
counselee would be helped by Confronting it. Confronting hurting people, who will often try to please,
can cause them to agree with the counselor's observations whether those observations are accurate or not. A
severely wounded counselee will often have a history of
being mistreated. For him, being dominated by others
is a lifestyle. Therefore, a counselor should question
his own motive before Confronting. And as mentioned
previously, Confronting should always be done with a
heart of tender compassion. Even when it's done well

Effective Listening

by a seasoned professional, Confrontation is still uncomfortable for most counselees. Sincere concern for
the counselee must be the motivating factor when applying this difficult listening skill.

Chapter IV

Conclusion

This concludes our discussion of Dialogue Skills. It is our prayer that you will practice these skills and apply them in your sessions. As you do so you will become a more Effective Listener. Everything you do well at this point in your life you have spent many hours, if not years, doing. If you are new to the counselor's role set some goals for yourself. Work toward those goals. You may not feel very confident now. And this is not unusual. It is because you lack experience. When you receive instruction and apply it in practical exercises you develop wisdom. Wisdom is a trait possessed by most successful counselors. The truly effective ones have learned how to help someone tell his story. They have learned how to go slow, build rapport, and use Open Questions. By applying the skills in this book you will become a better listener.

We have not attempted an exhaustive treatment of this subject. Many more pages could be filled discussing in detail the topics presented here. However, our intent has been to share some of the more useful Dialogue Skills and offer practical tips on implementing them in the counseling session. Don't hesitate to read other books on the subjects. Talk to other counselors. Ask them questions about how they run their sessions. Hopefully we have answered some of your questions.

We pray this discussion has caused many more questions to be asked. It is by applying these skills in the real sessions that you gain experience. Sometimes you

Effective Listening

will succeed and at times you might fail. All of us experienced counselors can share stories of our blunders!
But so goes the learning process. We all develop our
counseling skill as we go along. We encourage you to
practice with a partner and ask questions of those more
experienced than yourself.

May God bless your efforts in the work of helping Him
heal the brokenhearted and setting the captives free.

Appendices

Effective Listening

Appendix A

The Counseling Room

Comfort, Security, and Confidentiality

Many people have asked us over the years for advice about setting up a room or office for counseling. When planning a room or office for counseling keep your purpose in mind. The goal is to create an environment that helps the counselee feel safe, secure, and comfortable. The choice of location for counseling sessions as well as the appointments of the room can play a major part in the counselee's sense of comfort and security. The minimum requirement is to provide for sound security. Doors and walls should provide adequate insulation to keep the discussion private. Each session should be heard by no one other than those in the room. Nothing that is said in the room during the session should be spoken beyond the door after the session. As my favorite counseling professor, Betsy Kylstra, would say, "If you can't maintain confidentiality, find another line of work."

Furniture

Furniture should be comfortable because you're going to be sitting for long periods of time. Most counseling sessions last for at least one hour. When I was in private practice my sessions were ninety minutes. Using the Kylstra's RTF model the session is three hours. The counselee will be more comfortable in a love seat or couch than he will be seated on a chair. Either of the larger pieces gives a couple plenty of room during joint sessions. We try to put married couples in couches rather than chairs. If there are two counselors working as a team, separate chairs are a must.

When a table is necessary between the counselors and counselee keep it low and only as large as needed to hold the basic essentials like water glasses and a box of tissues. There should be enough room between the chairs and the table for everyone to cross their legs or stretch them out comfortably. Don't forget a waste basket for used tissues!

Many men are uncomfortable enough just being in the counseling session. So make them as comfortable as you can. If they are large they need furniture which gives them adequate support. Remember, they're going to be in those seats for as much as three hours per session. Multiply that by five or six sessions in the course of a typical week of RTF sessions and the comfort of those seats becomes extremely important.

Room Appointments

The room appointments, carpet, window treatment, wall decorations, can add to your counseling room either a sense of continuity or of chaos. The tone and mood of these details should exude comfort and relaxation. Colors should be complimentary. It's best if a color scheme is decided upon and worked out well in advance of your first session. Stay away from bright colors and too many colors. Soft soothing earth tones or light soft blues and greens are good choices. Prints or paintings should not portray people as subjects. Pastoral scenes and landscapes or seascapes are fresh every time you look at them. Try to reach a happy medium between feminine and masculine subjects, not too extreme either way, unless you have the luxury of creating different rooms for men and women.

Climate Control

Efficient climate control is a must; cool in the warmer months and warm in the cooler months. For the appliances the rule is; the quieter the better. A rattling window or wall air conditioner can be tolerated, but only if there is no other option. If overhead or floor fans are used they should operate with a minimum of noise.

Odors

Odors and toxicity are a consideration also. New carpet and most wall coverings and drapery materials and furniture fabric are treated with formaldehyde. Formaldehyde fumes are mildly toxic for most people and completely intolerable for others. Many new environmental illnesses and immune system disorders are a result of exposure to the toxic chemicals resident in various fabrics. It can take weeks to air them out. Be sure to air the room as long as needed for removing these toxins from the air. This may mean several days or in some cases even weeks! Don't plan your first session the day after new carpet is installed. You will be unpleasantly surprised!

Fast food breakfasts or lunches that are eaten in a counseling room or office can also leave offensive odors behind. Keep this in mind. Some people find the fragrance of sausage biscuits, grease burgers and onion rings intolerable. Believe it or not, even the smell of fresh perked coffee is offensive to some folks! If at all possible, refrain from eating foods with strong odors in the counseling room.

Effective Listening

These suggestions on the counseling room are offered in the interest of providing as much comfort and security as possible for the counselee. When setting up a counseling room or office for the first time, try to be flexible and content to work within your budget. However, if necessary, Effective Listening can be accomplished while sitting on the ground under a shade tree. The bottom line should be to glorify God in your work while making the counselee as secure and comfortable as possible.

Appendix B

The Parallel Journey

An important parallel exists between the process of sanctification and the spiritual and emotional healing sought by individuals who come for Christian counseling. It is in the best interest of the emotional, spiritual, and relational health of the counselor and the counselee to understand this parallel.

Healing and sanctification are both processes that can be likened to a parallel journey that continues throughout one's life. On this journey each individual is free to move at his own pace. He can stop along the way to admire the view. If he is taken with a particular vista he has the option to stay as long as he likes. Sometimes the trek is easy and delightful, at other times it is strenuous and down-right uncomfortable. Often there are trials along the way that cause the traveler to reconsider his reasons for embarking on the trip in the first place. During particularly difficult times along the road, he may even consider giving up his quest and turn back.

The Goal and The Destination

The destination of each of these parallel journeys is complete health. As for the sanctification journey, scripture teaches that the believer who "endures to the end" will eventually arrive at the place where he stands face to face with his risen Lord. At that time he will see his Lord as gloriously radiant as He truly is! In that incomparable moment the believer will also notice that he has been transformed. Just like his Lord, the believer will be perfect in every way, as God originally intended.

Physical and emotional well being became the holy grail in the 1990's. Physical fitness videos generate millions of dollars annually for their promoters, personal fitness trainers are big business, health clubs are found on every main street all over the world, and medical and nutritional self-help books stay on best sellers' lists for months. It appears as though the quest for holistic health currently in vogue will not slow down any time soon. Yet total health will not be apprehended until the heavenly destination is achieved! Until then the faithful must be steadfast in his journey. Therefore, continuing the journey should become the goal, whether it is in physical fitness, emotional health, or sanctification.

On the parallel journey the goal is different than the destination. The destination is a predestined point on a map of God's making. He knows where the finish line is and when the victory celebration will take place. Until then the goal in healing or sanctification is to continue the journey with the blessing of His guidance and power. Even when progress is painful or slow, encouragement is available if the individual keeps in mind the difference between the goal and the destination. The goal is to stay on the path, knowing the destination will be reached eventually.

The Journey Begins

The parallel journey of healing and sanctification begins when a man calls Jesus Christ, "Lord and Savior." In that moment of decision he changes his residence from the kingdom of darkness to the Kingdom of Light. Though the awakening of the need for a Savior and the time it takes to respond to God varies dramatically from one person to another, the result is the same. When a man is "reborn" he changes kingdoms. What lies ahead after being reborn is a life filled with opportunities to grow. The new-born child of God is on the path to become the healthy, loving individual God desires him to be.

When a man takes the oath of allegiance to Christ, he is responding to the call of God to become like Christ. A. W. Tozer[1] said the answer to the question, "What must I do to be saved?" is simply "to surrender to Christ, to get to know God personally, and to grow to become like Him." In Tozer's view a Christian is literally, "one who is becoming like Christ." The new believer who identifies himself with Christ does so as he submits himself to the process of becoming like Christ. This process is sanctification. In it's totality the word implies that two changes have taken place. First, a status has been conferred. The new believer is "holy," that is, separated from the world for God's service. Secondly, a process has begun. In this process the believer continually resists temptation, continues to repent, continues to seek forgiveness, and follows hard after God's will in all situations.

---

[1] Tozer, A. W., Please see Bibliography.

Sanctification and Healing

Prior to conversion a man does not function the way
God wants him to. He is deceived, impure, self cen-
tered, and destined to grow progressively worse. In the
Biblical sense he is a sinner. In that condition he is
doomed to destruction, hell is his inevitable destination,
and there is nothing he can do to change his condition.
From a clinical perspective the product of sin is sick-
ness. According to psychologist Alfred Adler,[1] "It is
the individual who is not interested in his fellow man
who has the greatest difficulties in life and provides the
greatest injury to others." With very few exceptions,
children, soon after birth, demonstrate self-centered behavior until they are corrected and disciplined. Even
when properly groomed and behaved though, the child
is still a sinner.

Through the grace of God in Jesus Christ, this pathetic
situation can be changed. A repentant individual can
enter through the small gate (Matthew 7:13-14) God
has provided and begin his healing/sanctifying journey.
As he repents he is forgiven for his crimes against God,
the penalty is paid by Christ, and he is granted eternal
fellowship with God. However, as good as this fellowship can be, redemption does not remove the repentant
individual from a sinful/sick environment. The sancti-
fying/healing journey is embarked upon against a rush-
ing tide of social ungodliness. The journey is filled
with trials and trouble at every turn in the road. These
tribulations continually impede and threaten to disrupt
the new believer's progress.

---

[1] Adler, Alfred, publication unknown.

Thankfully, God has not left the new believer alone in this decadent arena. Even though he is surrounded by his deadly enemies; sin, ungodly lifestyles, and demonic oppression, there is hope. For God has placed him in the compassionate care of His Holy Spirit. Even against the odds, by working in harmony with the Holy Spirit, the believer can steadily mature in the process of becoming like Christ. And eventually, at some predetermined point in the future known only by God, he will complete the sanctification process and arrive at the final and glorious destination!

The Spirit and the Counselor

The counselor's function in the counselee's healing journey is similar to the Holy Spirit's function in the sanctification process. In scripture the Holy Spirit is known as the comforter, the helper, and the Spirit of truth. His various tasks include but are not limited to guiding, comforting, strengthening, healing, and instructing. The believer is dependent upon the Holy Spirit to transform him, but it is essential that he invite and allow the Holy Spirit to develop his character to correspond to the image of Christ. Much like any other kind of growth, being transformed into the image of Christ is not an automatic process. It requires constant effort. There is much in our corrupt world that would keep us from becoming faithful and effective ambassadors for Christ.

Similarly, the counselor is invited by the counselee to come alongside the counselee just as the Holy Spirit does a new believer. The counselor may comfort, teach, or equip the counselee to overcome every obstacle he encounters on his journey through this sin/sick life toward health. The counselor might weep with him in his suffering and rejoice with him in his victories. He will offer Empathy in light of the counselee's hopelessness, bond with him in his loneliness, and accept him with all his shortcomings, inadequacies and ungodly behavior, attitudes, and speech. All this is done for the benefit of leading the counselee closer to God, so God can continue to heal him and empower him to keep moving along on the parallel journey.

This analogy between the Holy Spirit and the counselor does have limitations though. The work of the Holy Spirit is eternal. The work of the counselor is temporary. The counselor's work with the counselee is only for such time as is necessary to get the counselee moving again on his healing journey. The counselee may have lost contact with the Holy Spirit prior to the crisis that prompted his counseling appointment. Therefore, one of the tasks of the counselor may be to reconnect the counselee to the reality of the person and presence of the Holy Spirit. When this is done the counselee may once again begin moving forward toward the destination under his own power and in harmony with the Holy Spirit. At that point, the counselor's work is finished, but the work of the Holy Spirit continues until the believer is standing in a glorified body before the throne of God.

Bear in mind, dear Christian counselor, you are called by God to represent to the counselee the love, the mercy, and the grace of Almighty God. You are a fountain of forgiveness, pouring out to the wounded, the broken, the deceived, and the hopeless, the never ending, all sufficient grace of God. You are a department of transportation employee working the sometimes dark and difficult road of sanctification/ healing.

You shine His light to illuminate their path. Simply said, the purpose of "Christocentric" counseling is to reacquaint a malfunctioning man with the omnipotent and magnificent God.

Conclusion

Considering the significance of this parallel journey, he who answers the call to counsel should embrace his role soberly and humbly. It is an awesome responsibility to minister the restorative love of God to a counselee. The first concern is to possess this love. Before he offers a cup of refreshing to the thirsty counselee, the counselor must take it to the well to be filled. This means he must know God personally, be active in growing in Christ and have an ongoing, ever deepening relationship with the Holy Spirit. The first step for the Christian counselor is to be reconciled to God by receiving His grace through faith. The second step is to willfully and consistently continue along on his own healing/sanctifying journey.

Be assured, God can and will use whom He chooses. The counselor's weaknesses and need of spiritual maturity is not a hindrance to God. He is the one who can make the rocks burst forth with praise if need be! The stronger a counselor is in Him, the more effective he will be. If he is steadfast in prayer, knowledgeable of the Word, and living in harmony with His Spirit, the counselor's efforts will be rewarded, the counselee will benefit, and God will receive credit and praise for any and all healing that occurs!

Therefore, take heart fellow traveler. As you are reading these words, the destination remains somewhere up ahead. The road may yet have trials and temptations enough to cause the most dedicated traveler to consider turning back. But as sure as the ocean's waves continue to crash against the shore, he who continues his journey will arrive.

Appendix C

A Brief History of Christian Counseling Ministry

Counseling has been a part of the Christian experience since the beginning of time. When confronted with difficult decisions, men have always required and sought the counsel of those older or wiser. Since his days in the first Garden, in Eden, man has always had three sources of counseling wisdom; God, God's adversary, and himself.

In the Garden, man walked and talked with God in the cool of the day. They had direct contact with each other on a regular basis and, as the scripture indicates, all was well. But, for some reason still not fully understood by the author, the serpent was given access to the Garden and to man. Perhaps God wanted to find out (or to show man what would happen) if man would resist the temptation to take advice from someone whose counsel directly opposed the counsel of God. As we all know, Adam and Eve listened to, believed, and acted upon the advice of the serpent. And as we say, the rest is history!

Even though, to be spared eternal agony, they had to be evicted from the Garden, God continued to offer counsel to them. An example of this interaction is found in the story of Cain and Able. When Cain was troubled over being rejected God tried to help him by counseling him. He tried to help Cain see that his behavior, godly or ungodly, would bring about a corresponding result.

Effective Listening

Like his father before him, Cain rejected the counsel of God and chose to give in to the rage he held inside him. He murdered his brother, Able!

From Cain's sad experience through the flood and on until the story of Abraham, scripture shows how God continued to give counsel to various men. Always His goal was to help mankind live in peaceful harmony with His divine plan. This was so man could enjoy his life as much as possible even though he struggled to live happily in a world that had become corrupt by Adam's original sin.

Since the day Adam rejected the counsel of God, history shows that there has always existed a natural process whereby men with problems seek the advice and counsel of those reputed to be wiser than themselves.

History has testified that God has always desired and attempted to give man advice that would make man's life more comfortable. God knows that when we do it His way life is generally good. When we do it our way life is, well, never mind. The biblical record gives glaring examples of this in nearly every book of the Bible. The story of Moses, the leader of Israel, is one very good example. Perhaps this is the beginning of Christian counseling as we know it.

Moses was falling apart under the pressure of trying to counsel the tribe. Jethro told Moses he could not counsel all the people all the time. Their needs were too numerous and too diverse. And attempting to do so was going to send Moses to an early grave, before they reached the promised land! Moses happily agreed and set up a system whereby all the people received counsel from a hierarchy of counselors.

The family of man in every era has had access to godly counsel. From the time of Moses until the early twentieth century this counsel has been primarily available through the services of religious institutions!

It was not until the advent of Freudian psychotherapy early in the twentieth century that the church began to doubt the effectiveness of a biblical counseling approach. With the birth of the modern psychology movement the church and the general public was offered a new counseling model. Academics and intellectuals began to promote the merits of a new discipline called, psychology. Their new theory promoted the idea that man's mind was the ruler of his soul and body. And that his mind was a mysteriously complicated maze of emotional impulses that only highly skilled professionals could understand. This theory is probably not too far from the truth. However, in psychology, as in any discipline, diagnosing a problem is only the beginning. The real work is finding an effective solution to the problem!

It is interesting to note the definition of psychology and psychotherapy. These terms are a combination of two root words from the Greek. Psych comes from the Greek root word for soul, the unseen part of man. Therapy comes from the Greek root therapuos (sp) which means care and is used interchangeably with, cure. Ology means the study of... as in psychology, theology, biology, etc. The point is, soul care or cure, and the study of it, should be the work of professionals who hold a christocentric world view. To effectively diagnose, treat, and heal the soul/mind/spirit of man, one needs a revelation from God regarding the true nature of man's makeup. One would never expect to repair a car's engine without the owner's manual. Why then did the church turn the repair of man's spirit, soul, and mind over to those who did not understand the designer's original plan? The mistake the church made was to throw the baby out with the bath water. With the advent of the modern psychological movement the church gave all of its problems over to the trained professionals. When really it needed only to refer its most difficult cases to psychologists.

But, the reader may argue, "just because we are members of the church does not mean we possess the skill to engage in soul care." True. But if we know the creator and believe He is who He says He is, we know also He can teach us to provide effective diagnosis and treatment for all but the most difficult psychological, emotional, and relational problems. The truth is, the majority of Church counseling issues are relational. Husbands and wives conflict, parents and children conflict, etc.

The most effective Christian counselor and the best psychologist will be the one who knows God personally and as a result, possesses an understanding of the true nature of God and the true nature of man.

Since the Charismatic renewal began in the early 1960's the church has debated, sometimes fiercely, the merits of Christian counseling. In their efforts to treat the body of Christ there have been errors made by well meaning but untrained Christian counselors. Their excesses and sometimes far-out theories have not always helped the cause. And they have had a plethora of critics both within and outside the church. However, during the past two decades the church has once again openly embraced it's God ordained responsibility for soul care. The sensitive and intelligent writing of Gary Collins, Larry Crabb, James Dobson, and a host of others have helped all of us reclaim our former territory.

At the present time things look good for those seeking Christian counseling. All over the world, qualified highly skilled Christian counselors are very busy helping the Holy Spirit bring healing to the broken hearted.

If you feel called to this most humbling profession we urge you to soak your desire to counsel in prayer. The effective Christian counselor is a man or woman who pursues God in prayer. There is no better teacher than the Holy Spirit and secondly, other spirit-filled counselors. Read all you can find on counseling psychology. Study God's word. To be the best counselor you can be, you must know God and you must know His Word.

To be any good at all you must develop a counseling theory of your own. It must be based on the writing of those who have gone on before you. Don't be afraid to read Christian psychology. You don't need to re-invent the wheel. Many dedicated Christians have led the way for us who follow in their footsteps. Clyde Narramore, Archibald Heart, Gary Collins, and others have given us a library filled with great books on the subject of Christian psychology and counseling.

It is our fervent prayer that you will find, follow and fulfill God's wonderful destiny for your life. For those who do are indeed blessed. And their lives will be a blessing. For there are no better words to hear than "well done good and faithful servant."

May God bless richly you and your efforts.

Effective Listening

Bibliography

1. Collins, Gary, *How To Be A People Helper*, Regal Books, Ventura CA, 1976.

    In this small volume Dr. Collins has given the Christian community a real good introduction to counseling. It supports some of the material presented in Effective Listening and is recommended without reservation as an easily read presentation on the why and how of Christian counseling. And if you can find a copy of this author's The Rebuilding of Psychology, get it.

2. Crabb, Larry, *Finding God*, Zondervan, Grand Rapids MI, 1993.

    Larry Crabb has become a major voice in the Christian counseling community. He has written several excellent and popular books. In this volume he candidly exposes his personal pain and reveals his own healing journey. Very encouraging for those embarking on a similar healing journey.

3. Haugk, Kenneth, *Christian Care Giving, A Way of Life*, Augsburg Publishing House, Minneapolis MN, 1984.

    Another small but important look at Christian care-giving.

4. Kylstra, Chester and Betsy, *Restoring the Foundations, Second Edition*, Proclaiming His Word, Inc., Santa Rosa Beach FL, 1994, 1996, 2001.

   This book presents an in depth view of the integrated model of Biblical counseling developed by Chester and Betsy Kylstra. It is highly recommended for anyone interested in an innovative, thorough, and truly scriptural model of counseling.

5. Tozer, A. W., *The Pursuit of God*, Christian Publications, Camp Hill, PA, 1948.

   I must confess, everything I write about God, Jesus Christ, the Holy Spirit, or counseling, has been influenced by the writings of A.W. Tozer. If I were to ask any Christian to read any one book in addition to his or her Bible, this is it. The author will present your Heavenly Father to you in such illuminating light that you will run to your prayer closet to sit in the healing Silence of God's glorious love. Read it and be blessed.

Effective Listening

Effective Listening

Effective Listening

CPSIA information can be obtained
at www.ICGtesting.com
Printed in the USA
FFOW02n2223170416
23259FF